HUMAN HOURS

Also by Catherine Barnett

Into Perfect Spheres Such Holes Are Pierced
The Game of Boxes

HUMAN HOURS

POEMS ◆ CATHERINE BARNETT

Graywolf Press

This publication is made possible, in part, by the voters of Minnesota through a Minnesota State Arts Board Operating Support grant, thanks to a legislative appropriation from the arts and cultural heritage fund, and a grant from the Wells Fargo Foundation. Significant support has also been provided by Target, the McKnight Foundation, the Lannan Foundation, the Amazon Literary Partnership, and other generous contributions from foundations, corporations, and individuals. To these organizations and individuals we offer our heartfelt thanks.

Published by Graywolf Press
250 Third Avenue North, Suite 600
Minneapolis, Minnesota 55401

www.graywolfpress.org

Published in the United States of America

ISBN 978-1-55597-814-3

2 4 6 8 9 7 5 3

Library of Congress Control Number: 2018934481

Cover design: David Wells

Cover art: Eve Sussman

Contents

◆

◆

◆

◆

◆

HUMAN HOURS

The Amenities

Enchantée, says the key in my hand.
When I try to turn it, it turns to sand.

Time is an upgrade, says the front desk,
reserved for our most valued guests.

Time is an anemone, says the new hire.
Enemy. Amenity. Profanity. Dire.

Whatever you've forgotten,
they provide. Loved one,

plotline, packet of minutes?
Glass eyes, false teeth, all sleep is gratis.

How sweet
we look in our hotel linens.

En Route

Alone in Siena, I bought a bottle of elixir,
Elisire di S. Caterina.
The basilica was closing, though the lights
were still bright in the side chapel,
the marble chapel where Catherine's head

is mummified, set in a scalloped case,
behind a grille, under lock and key,
far from her body still buried in Rome.
For a few minutes I stood there,
trying to understand. Was she art or fact?

The man next to me was running his fingers
through his hair. Breathing.
Volatile organic compound poorly lit
beside the gilt reliquary.

It seemed like the right time for resolutions.
Patience, urgency, forgiveness, acceptance.
Elixirs should be kept in clocks.
Made of bergamot and fumes,

this one spreads furtively across the dawn
and burns when I drink it down like spirits.

An Apprehension

Ten below, high of zero, 4:11 p.m.
flashed the alarm panel's handsome blue touchscreen.

Without commotion or fire the afternoon
passed slowly, full of promise,

then disappointment.
Without heartbreak or break-in.

For company I had Kafka on my lap
and Qolsys vibrating lightly against the wall.

4:34 . . . 4:35 . . .
There are all sorts of creatures in the world, I read,

wretched, limited, dumb creatures
who have no language but mechanical cries.

I stood up and stretched.
Face to face with Qolsys,

I peered into the sensors, into the little hole
of the siren, and touched up my lipstick.

Maybe I can ask Dave to come back, I thought,
Dave from Royal Security,

Dave with the smoky brown eyes,
maybe he can help.

I took off my slippers,
my bargain-basement bra, and danced.

Silence. Not even a mechanical cry—
I wondered if the fault were mine.

Maybe I miswired the hard data?
The soft data?

Maybe the poor thing simply had no loins.
I opened the window.

Window opening, said Qolsys
in a deep male voice.

Outside there were heavy birds
weighing down the winter trees,

heaps of them in the gloaming, almost purple,
waiting for what, who can say?

I shut the window.
Window closing, said Qolsys.

It was a start, not so very different from others of my species,
narrating events as they happen,

I'm coming,
I'm coming—

I opened the window again,
letting the cold air press across my wrists,

the back of my neck, my lips, hoping
at least the motion detector, inside,

or the birds, outside,
would respond to the scent that pulsed there.

You will not go unsampled! I heard the birds say.
Be mine! I heard the trees say.

I could have turned down the sound,
I could have shut the window,

but like a darkness slowly advancing,
like winter lightning,

we are drawn together.

The Light from across the Fields

Past the laundromat and the empty church,
down Cedar Lane to where the road peters out,
I drove into the woods and there it was,
shining like the human mind.

Under it was an old car I'd seen parked
at the Quiet Man Bookshop.
So it was his light.
Are you moving? he'd asked once

when I came by his store with books to give away.
Lots of people ask me that,
I don't know why.
Are you moving? said the cashier at Marshalls

when I rolled my cart up to the counter
with four new pillows
and what looked like a man thrown inside.
The mind, yes, is always moving.

Tonight everything in the world
seems to be asleep except that light,
that light and this blanket slipping to the floor
as if it, too, wants to run off somewhere.

The Skin of the Face Is That Which Stays Most Naked, Most Destitute

But it's in perfectly fine shape, the face in the mirror said—

When I first acquired you, yes, ok, years ago,
on a lark, and you were just something to wear then,
to the store, or the park, not alone in the dark.

Forensics

For a few years I studied the faces of malefactors and con men.
The quick zigzag of the colonel,

for example, who took pictures of himself
in his victims' lingerie.

I was mesmerized by such dioramas,
having fallen in love with one once

a long time ago,
and can still picture the vermillion border,

the lips and hands that debouched right into me
who must have wanted to be misled.

Now my eyebrow is perpetually raised,
I can't bring it down.

I changed lovers,
changed the lock on my front door,

locked the car where there were no signs
of intrusion other than my missing clothes

and the passenger door left open
on the city street where I'd parked.

Only he and I had the key,
which is lost now

and cannot be duplicated.
Do not resuscitate, I say to my mind.

Do not duplicate.
Dupe, we say as verb and noun.

Sounds like what it is, what I am—
I hope the city where this happened

has filed the truth somewhere in its archives.
Who'll tell the other stories?

Not I, say the lampposts.
Not I, say the dogs.

Not I, says the I
who's scanned everything

and scanned the scans onto memory cards
and locked the memory cards in a safety-deposit box.

I did it late at night
as if I were the criminal

and maybe I was, and am.
Often I dreamed he dismembered someone,

hid her in the walls,
and in these dreams I was participant and observer

as I am again now, dreaming of writing this.

Epistemology

Mostly I'd like to feel a little less, know a little more.
Knots are on the top of my list of what I want to know.
Who was it who taught me to burn the end of the cord
to keep it from fraying?
Not the man who called my life a debacle,
a word whose sound I love.
In a debacle things are unleashed.
Roots of words are like knots I think when I read the dictionary.
I read other books, sure. Recently I learned how trees communicate,
the way they send sugar through their roots to the trees that are ailing.
They don't use words, but they can be said to love.
They might lean in one direction to leave a little extra light for another tree.
And I admire the way they grow right through fences, nothing
stops them, it's called *inosculation*: to unite by openings, to connect
or join so as to become or make continuous, from *osculare*,
to provide with a mouth, from *osculum*, little mouth.
Sometimes when I'm alone I go outside with my big little mouth
and speak to the trees as if I were a birch among birches.

Still Life

Could it have been the doctor's kind manner
and eyes that distracted me long enough
for him to lift the rubber tube from the metal tray
and ask me to lick it? Which I did.

For a moment I thought that might be it,
fiber-optic laryngoscopy was like oral sex
on a very thin penis with a camera for a head,
painless, until without explanation

or forewarning the doctor slid the tiny camera
up through my nose and down into my throat.
Holy fuck, I said, when I saw the screen
where the origins of the self were splayed.

Hadn't I wanted to be known like that?
Seen from the inside, lit from within
like the intimacies of *L'Origine du monde*,
a painting I love because it makes

beautiful what I've mostly kept hidden
in shame. Cunt, some of you have called it,
or God, pulsing there in the small gilt frame.

Landscape with Borrowed Contours

If you've got it, flaunt it,
said a t-shirt my mother gave me,
but what did I have?

Tiny batteries in my breasts,
which hummed along, expectant.
I did and didn't want to grow up

and into a woman
so I tore pages out of *Mademoiselle*
and the monthlies we found hidden

under our fathers' medical journals,
photos I studied as I cut out a CV
of eyes, mouths,

legs, hips, lips, nipples.
What did I have?
Farrago messages,

tomboy's body, irreconcilable gig
of what it meant to be "liberated."
More nipples than clouds, more clouds

than faces, more faces than mothers.
I worked my way around each silhouette,
made a collage,

and shellacked the whole rig with glue
until it crazed, an amateur's map
once but no longer kept pinned

beside the full-length mirror
out of which unrecognizable landscape
I sometimes stare.

Lyric and Narrative Time at Café Loup

Has it passed quickly or slowly? the young women asked
with eerie timing—

At exactly that moment an old astonished cockroach
crawled out from the spring salad laid before me

and walked like a creosote angel across the white cloth.
The women must have seen me blanch or the waiter

sweep clean the table with a piece of fresh warm bread.
What was it? they asked,

What happened?
What was it?

The most pressing questions are naive.
For example, who invented hours? Who stole the hair from your head?

Whenever I see a bald spot I want to shout a little,
in praise. Such ephemera between my salty legs—

Time is one part of the body that never gets washed.
All those moments between the neurons!

Where are you going? the women asked, though I'd hardly moved.
Where are you hurrying to?

Accursed Questions, i

A doctor suggested I spend four minutes a day asking questions about whatever matters most to me.

Four minutes, that's how long it takes to boil an egg, get from 96th to 42nd on the express train, initiate an irreversible apocalypse.

How do I get out of here? is the question my father asks most frequently. It takes him three or four seconds to say the seven syllables, there are frequent glitches in his speech but it's a perfect mantra.

What next? and Jackie? are his other inquiries.

Jackie what next Jackie what next Jackie—

If you count repetitions, they add up to at least four minutes.

At dinner I asked my mother which wh-question she'd keep if she could use only one, and she said *why*.

I remember when she first told me she reads the obits to see how old people are when they die. A young man was recently in love with her, but she stayed loyal to my father, who's lost his memory. He doesn't ask who we are but often he wonders if we have something to do with him. Oh that's grand, he says when I explain who I am to him, and he to me.

Each time I read *He will never ride the red horse she describes* I feel sad until I remember the red horse is the sun, the same sun that will rise too soon tomorrow morning right here over my left shoulder.

My son is sleeping on the couch with all the lights on. Nothing bad can happen.

How long does it take? he says in his sleep.

———

Lying together a friend and I tried just to speak in questions. It was as intimate a way of passing time as any, except sex, I think. He asked why I have two empty glass bowls on the bookshelf. I didn't answer because I was only listening.

When my son was little, they were filled with Halloween candy.

———

What is an ending? the students sometimes ask. Ah, the answer to that question brings the priest and the doctor running over the hills.

———

Maybe best not to ask when will what take whom where and to do what.

Jean once told me she's not interested in writing about getting older but about getting dead. In *Lucy*, she speaks directly to the oldest and most complete human ancestor. There is no boundary between the living and the dead:

> Or what do you do now Lucy
>
> for love?
> Your eye-holes.

Those of us who are scared just chronicle the slow path. The scar where they pulled my son from me is starting to sag now, etc., etc.

Turns out *when* is a question children learn late, after *where*, *what*, and *who*. *Why* is perhaps the latest, and it can go on incessantly.

Why and *when* and *where* and *what* all go back to the root *who*.

Lately I've been walking around talking to myself, who is full of swearing and disbelief.

Without much hope I opened my first small bottle of 3-in-One oil and applied it to the hinges of my front door that apparently keep my neighbor up at night. Squirting the oil on the wildly overpainted hinge was like throwing seeds on a blacktop and expecting a garden. But it worked, and that cheered me up.

Imagine if Augustine had been addressing 3-in-One oil instead of God:

> Do the heaven and earth then contain Thee, since Thou fillest them? or dost Thou fill them and yet overflow, since they do not contain Thee? And whither, when the heaven and the earth are filled, pourest Thou forth the remainder of Thyself? . . . Oh! that Thou wouldest enter into my heart, and inebriate it, that I may forget my ills, and embrace Thee, my sole good!

Can't we let him sleep all winter?

He wants to be set free. He wants to be set free upon the waters.

So much depends upon the kindness of questions. And the questions we cannot not speak of.

The radio is playing "Blowin' in the Wind," which was one of the first songs I learned on the guitar. At the age of ten, I couldn't get enough of the questions. I played it for anyone who'd listen, I played it in my nightgown, in my hand-me-down red Speedo, in my mother's sunglasses, in the reflection in my father's martini glass. I got so good at it I could play it while balancing on a bongo board in the middle of the living room. I got so good at it I can still feel the precariousness underfoot.

Appeal to Numbers

In the brief rented rooms of our randomized
uncontrolled experiment

nights seem to last longer when I count
one Mississippi two Mississippi

not doing much
only watching you sleep now

your mouth a little bit open
my mouth a little bit open

Why are you so uneducated you once asked
It's true I can't read music charts spreadsheets

the future the signs the leaves your face
the racing forms

But stats ok yes
Statistic of impermanence

statistic of desire
YOU WERE HERE

says the silvery green light of time
breathing in and out like any mortal

eight Mississippi nine—

Comic Morning

What's funny about this place
is us regulars coming in with our different
accoutrements, mine lately the little void
of space I call honey, days
I can barely get through I'm laughing so hard,
see? In the back a woman squeezes oranges,
someone presses the fresh white bread
into communion wafers or party favors.
In the window the chickens rotate blissfully,
questioning nothing—
Sometimes I flirt with the cashier, just improvising,
the way birds land all in a hurry on the streetlamp,
which stays warm even on cold nights.
Guillaume says humor is sadness
and he's awfully pretty.
What do they put in this coffee? Men?
No wonder I get a little high. Remember
when we didn't have sex on the Ferris wheel,
oh that was a blast,
high, high above the Tuileries!

Idée Fixe

No woman wants to be low-hanging fruit,
my glamorous girlfriend says, but I'm indiscriminate
and love all fruit, I'm tempted to list each kind
right here, in and out of season,
because even just saying the names gives me pleasure,
as does saying your name.
I'm not alone in my passion—my whole family,
we're a little off in this regard,
we can spend hours talking about cantaloupe
or arguing over how many flats to buy
when it's Peach-O-Rama at the Metropolitan.
Once I even drove half a day to get to Pence Orchards
where I met and took photos of Bert Pence,
who sold me three boxes of peaches at a wholesale price.
He was so good to me, as was the late-summer freestone
I picked as I walked back through the orchard
in the August heat to the entrance gates,
which were nothing like the Gates of Hell.
On the contrary, I was in heaven there in Yakima.
I can still smell that single peach, which was profusely
low-hanging, it was the definition of low-hanging,
it fell into my hands, as you did—
or perhaps as I did into yours—
but that was months ago.
When I walked past the stands yesterday,
on what should have been the first day of spring,
all produce had been covered with heavy blankets,
to keep it warm, to mitigate harm.
Today the temperature dropped so low
someone thought to remove the fruit entirely and stash it away.
With this strange weather we're having, will I see you again?
I can't help myself.

Essay on *An Essay Concerning Human Understanding*

John Locke says children don't understand elapsed time,
and when I was a girl it was true
and it remains true—

It's been three hundred years and still my feelings for Locke
must pass unrequited.
I keep his book in my satchel

with other pleasures—
lipstick, Ricola, matches, binder clips, and a tiny bar of soap
stolen from the Renaissance Inn

where I sometimes cheat on Locke with another man.
At least objects endure—
see how my old sofa holds up!

Locke would look pretty good lying here
with his long face, his furrowed brow and center part,
he who too quickly flourished

and outraced this crowded place.
La duration, I said, trying to roll my *r*
when some new French friends asked

what I'd been thinking about.
John Locke et la duration.
They thought I said *l'adoration*,

which is also true.
Turns out *duration* is not a French word,
no matter how badly I pronounce it.

The correct term is *la durée*,
another word I mispronounce
though once I passed a lovely *durée*

riding my rented Vélib' from the Seine
to the Sacré-Coeur,
where had I planned in advance

I could have spent the night in adoration.
Instead I only leaned my bike against the church
and looked out across the sea of human hours.

Son in August

Dignity, I said to myself
as he carried his last things into the dorm.
It was not a long goodbye,

nothing sad in it,
all I had to do was turn
and head up the hill.

All I had to do was balance
on two feet that seemed to belong
to a marionette who had no idea

what came next or who governed the strings.
There's no emergency, I told her,
just get back to your car,

that's it, that's all that's required.
I didn't mind accompanying her,
I myself had nowhere to go.

She drove east then farther east
under a river through a tunnel
until she found herself back at home,

with a purpose.
And the purpose was?
To recognize the green awning.

To find a key in a pocket.
To fit that key in the lock,
take off her shoes, drop them on the floor

with others left there like old coins
from a place she must have visited.
Worth something but what.

There were no clues in the medicine cabinet,
none in the cupboard, none in the freezer
where she found old licorice and Bit-O-Honey

shoved next to a ziplock of bluish breast milk,
all of it frozen solid over nineteen years
into some work of art, a sculpture,

an archaic something of something.
She looked at my hands reaching into the freezer.
Or I looked at hers.

They were strong, worn, spackled with age
as they removed the milk-ice
stashed like weed far in the back.

Do they even make this stuff anymore?
What's it good for?
What was it ever good for?

Repurposed, she thought,
isn't that the word the kids keep saying
these days? Hey sweetie,

she called to the unoccupied room,
hey love. It was so hot the air
from the freezer turned to steam

and she took the ice into her own hands,
held it, held it gently against the back
of my warm animal neck

until something began to melt and I was alone.

Lore

To think, to swear, and to jaywalk I learned from my father,
who even now curses me if, his hand in mine,
I want to wait at the crosswalk.
I don't think waiting is such a dumb thing to do,
but my father has other opinions.
He's a thinking-man's jaywalker,
he's a thinking-man's thinking man
who can no longer think,
an emeritus who loved taking us to the Oasis
where we could borrow his penknife
and carve any profanities we liked into the long dark bar.
Shit, I'd like to carve there now. Or *Please explain!*
Back at home he taught us little about the US tax code
but showed us how to tie knots, pack a car, remove
the washcloths our mother placed gently over our eyes
when we took our first showers.
Some things were inimitable, beyond a child's capacities.
He moved his scalp back and forth with élan
when we asked him to flex his muscles.
Claimed he transplanted the hair from his head to his chest,
which I have yet to try.
Preserve your options, he often said.
Put me out on the ice, he often said, as he grew older until he grew older.
Adversity is when a hero's two options are both bad.
What's next, he says.
And then, he says.
What is wrong, he says and then forgets what he wanted to ask.
Old age is so profane.
When I waited tables, my father told me to declare my tips,
which I never did. I wore a floppy hat
and worked under the table.
Now I stand here with him dodging cars
as if they, too, like him are only desperate engines
saying slow down, or hurry along now.

The Necessary Preoccupations

Cure means something else to a roofer, as does *cant*.
I just found out I've got no mansard and my underlayment is aging
like my flashing, which were my eyes.
Eyes has the word *yes* in it, have you ever realized that?
I might have misheard the roofer's blue eyes.
Is there plywood on that baby? he asked.
And something about ferrule and bitumen,
a word I imagine having been called under as many roofs
as breaths. I like to say it with the British pronunciation.
Bitumen.
Hot stuff is bitumen, actually, I looked it up.
I look up but can't see the roof and can't climb up on the roof
to see the stars, which were his eyes.
Weep hole is not an anatomical term,
we looked for my weep holes but he couldn't find them,
he gave up too soon, some men do.
Doggedness is my hobby, that's what I wrote
on the jury-duty questionnaire.
Someone else wrote down happy hour.
Happy hours, which were his eyes—
He promised to send a bid last night but nothing
except *Your pkg has shipped*
came across the ether, through the skies,
down through the three layers of old shingles I've got to haul away
before anything new goes up.
Most shingles have a lifetime warranty now.
Who needs a lifetime?
All of *Ulysses* takes place in one single bitumen flashpoint of a day.
I see the words *yes* and *yeses* and *eyes* in *Ulysses*.
Molly Bloom says *yes* eighty-seven times and the sky touches the roof.
Yes, I would have said.
In the package coming my way are new headlights.
Those are headlights that were his eyes!
And blue-tinted headlights aren't even legal.

The Art of the Security Question

I love orange in the fall, maroon all winter.
Bach's cello suites, Nina Simone's "Ain't Got No."
My first kiss?
My father's mother's maiden name?
We just got scammed out of four thousand dollars.
Someone called and said my nephew,
caught DUI, needed to be bailed out.
Because we've already lost two children,
my mother and my sister went to every CVS in West Seattle
looking for enough gift cards to satisfy the man
who pretended he was in a Sacramento courtroom trying to help.
What do you think happens to you when you die?
my mother asked a week later.
What's that? asked my father, turning over in his sleep.
Researchers say the safest questions have answers that are not enduring.
If you asked me now what song I love best?
I like the soundtrack to *Call Me by Your Name*.
I sat next to my father in the movie theater.
Did he wonder why the stranger to his left
put her head on his shoulder?
He kept asking, Who's here with me?
Could that be a security question?
I ask myself if this is the last time.

O Esperanza!

Turns out my inner clown is full of hope.
She says she wants a gavel.
She wants to stencil her name on a wooden gavel:
Esperanza's Gavel.
Clowns are clichés and they aren't afraid of clichés.
Mine just sleeps when she's tired.
But she can't shake the hopes.
She's got a bad case of it, something congenital perhaps.
Maybe it was sexually transmitted,
something to do with oxytocin or contractions or nipple stimulation,
maybe that's it, a little goes a long way.
Hope is also the name of a bakery in Queens.
And there's a lake in Ohio called Hope Lake where you can get nachos.
I'm so stuffed with it the comedians in the Cellar never call on me,
even when I'm sitting right there in the front row with a dumb look of hope
     on my face.
Look at these books: hope.
Look at this face: hope.
When I was young I studied with Richard Rorty, that was lucky,
I stared out the window and couldn't understand a word he said,
he drew a long flat line after the C he gave me,
the class was called Metaphysics and Epistemology,
that's eleven syllables, that's
hope hope hope hope hope hope hope hope hope hope hope.
Just before he died, Rorty said his sense of the holy was bound up with the hope
that someday our remote descendants will live in a global civilization
in which love is pretty much the only law.

Accursed Questions, ii

I can't stop reading *Happy Days*. It's so perfect I understand it no better than the theory of relativity or the meaning of love hand-painted on signs held long ago by students down on the campus where we sometimes skinny-dipped in the fountain and stole fancy pens from the bookstore, genuine Montblancs that still don't work.

Guaranteed . . . genuine . . . pure . . . what? Winnie asks over and over in the first act, as if knowing will help between the bell for waking and the bell for sleep.

One weekend between the bells you and I kissed and kissed and the questions begin again.

Oh let them last at least until we are decanted from the vessel containing the fluid of future time to the vessel containing the fluid of past time, agitated by the phenomena of hours.

Are you allowed to ask that question? he said midmorning with the blinds drawn.

Yes, I nodded, but instead I asked, What are days for?

In the space between interlocutor and addressee, there is something erotic, responsive, uncontrolled.

No one likes to be interrogated, though I have to admit I have sometimes enjoyed being frisked. It hasn't happened in a while. In fact, recently I was allowed to pass through security without taking off my shoes. The man behind me wore boots I thought I could love, so I waited for him at the exit, pretending I was just tying up my flip-flop. Flimsy and inappropriate for where we were both headed.

I have always, all of my life, writes Elizabeth Hardwick in *Sleepless Nights*, been looking for help from a man.

As the boots glided past, I tried to think of a question, any question, a question for my thoughts.

―――

On a first date, my dinner companion seemed bemused I was doing all the asking. Sorry! I said. I can be quiet, I'd like that.

Then it was nice listening in to other conversations, noticing the sweat on the water glass, letting time pass all on its own, sipping a little wine while he ate more squid.

What do you want to ask me now, he said after a few slow bites, that you didn't want to ask me before?

―――

The interrobang was invented just a few decades ago and is a mark I've never been tempted to use though it's mostly what my eyes say.

Four minutes‽ Is that a long kiss?

Were you a piece of punctuation, wouldn't you just love to be the sexy little round black curve of the question pressed up against a lanky exclamation,

like this‽

Even pressed against you I'm trying to read lips.

The closer you are to your addressee the more fragile language is.

―――

It took me a long afternoon to memorize Shakespeare's *When in disgrace with fortune and men's eyes*. Sitting in my old car on Roosevelt Island watching my son play baseball, I felt the ache that comes when you commit something beautiful to heart. Then I looked through the rest of the sonnets and counted. I saw nine others begin with *when*.

When I think of *when*, I think of the simple one-word question.

If I don't dawdle, don't pause between recitations, don't get up and start making dinner or rereading your old letters, I can recite Sonnet 29 four times in four minutes.

Starting when? Now.

It's amazing. For someone who thinks she's so smart. Until this very moment, I thought *haply I think on thee* meant *happily*—

—

Why did I so rarely mention love when we were holding each other?

Does Anbesol work on the heart or only on the mind?

Did I misuse everything?

Did Kant really have a parrot?

What was the punch line?

Are sex and death the only rafts out of here?

Where did we think we were going?

—

Unasked questions between us all.

The Humanities

A classmate and I chose pendulums,
what happens when a pendulum

hangs from a pendulum?
How does gravity work then?

We were studying invisible forces
and left the classroom, heading into

the world with just our two bodies,
which were to be both string and bob.

In the woods behind school, he climbed into a tree
and lowered himself down,

holding a branch.
I reached up to his thin ankles

and lifted my bare feet off the ground.
Someone must have been there to try to make us swing,

record the harmonic oscillations,
and take the polaroids,

still stapled to this yellowed lab report.
It's haunting to discover it now, to see in the photos

how we hung there smiling, white,
safe and dumb.

How little history we knew.
If only all feet could come back

to stand on the ground,
not get buried under it,

left to hang above, left outside
in the told and untold,

in the toll of hot municipal suns.
We didn't understand much of anything

but completed the assignment,
typed up the results, passed physics,

went to college and typed and typed
and never took another science class,

we were humanities majors.
Sometimes when I'm not typing now

I run lines with an actor friend
and can't get them out of my head.

Another heavenly day,
says Winnie as the curtain rises.

She's buried to her waist in earth
and for a while you think it can't get any worse.

The humanities.
What are they, really?

Don't let me sleep on.

Calamity Jane on Etsy after the 2016 Election

As we lay together under the gabled roof, a lover
called me solicitous. That's me,

I thought, straightening my mussed-up hair,
Solicity Jane, anxious version

of Calamity Jane, the only female action figure to show up
on the UPS truck filled with soldiers and presidents

manufactured by my grandfather and sent out west
to my sisters and brother and me.

We were only five of his many grandchildren,
five kids who wanted to make-believe.

Often I find her at vintage stores, priced out of my range,
but today Calamity's cheap,

lying face down in the Etsy pixels.
Blond, wearing turquoise blue and an empty lasso,

she doesn't look a thing like me
unless you count the pose.

Right about now I want to wake up.
I want a round of shots, straight up.

And one for all my sisters,
and one for all my brothers.

And one for all my mothers.
At least she's only polymer.

No man can grab her by the smooth blue patina
between her unspreadable legs.

How long will she be lying here?
As I find myself again now,

saying god help us into the fitted sheet.
Hey, you there, Calamity, wake up!

It's not too late to fight back.
Calamity et al!

Get up, we love you!
I solicit you!

Calamity ends with amity,
amity save us all.

Another Divine Comedy

It's not age or cold or shame
or even the promise of heaven,
the proof of hell

that makes my sturdy self-lubricating relic
shake as it glides down Broadway
on this narrow ultra-low-resistance scooter.

No matter how hard I push,
I can't outrun the news,
can't stop the trucks, destruction, blood,

ICE, uranium, plutonium, floods.
I ride so wildly now it's like surfing.
I'm afraid to look down,

afraid to look back up.
I used to think the cries were only in my head,
but no.

That was logic.
Now I hear them in the wheels' raucous junket
down the avenues.

I hear them issuing from the manholes,
from the towers, from the cosmos
tossed in the way of the truck

as if we were no hardier than flowers.
Have mercy on us.
No hardier than flowers!

Let Facts Be Submitted to a Candid World

The facts aren't quiet and the facts weren't calm.
They're like weeds that even cut down to the root still flourish,
sending shouts up through whatever kept trying to smother us.
All of you, said the new president,

All of you have got to go, you're ruining us.
He tried to graffiti his name everywhere,
he tried to graft it everywhere,
even here, in the aftermath, in the wake of facts

never sleeping but only resting, pretending a death,
like the female moorland hawker falls from the sky
to avoid harassment then lifts up again,
like rhizomes cold hard drunk in winter soil

each spring rise up like the impossible promise,
like the derelict premise
I wrote down again at the top of this page,
copied verbatim from an earlier declaration,

might look like—look up—
like tombstone or horizon.

Metaphor on the Crosstown

A man carries an armful of dogwood into the bus,
into the pluribus, the branches wrapped
in the day's paper, the news no longer legible
but scrapped, reused, dampened, darkened,
waterlogged, bleeding. What was it

we thought we could go on reading?
Civility, justice, the First Amendment.
We look him over, as if to ask what he is meant
to mean carrying his dogwood into our crowded bus,
wrapped in poor passing facts and alive, furiously, like us.

Summons

Do I have a Certificate of Good Conduct,
Justice Milton Tingling wants to know.

I don't think I do, no—
For years I asked the court for exemptions

and when I did serve I was useless,
I didn't care about the chiropractor and his wife,

about theft, delinquency, malfeasance.
Justice was a beautiful

abstraction I counted on from within the walls
of my exhausted mothermind.

It's a long time since I've been summoned,
and now Milton Tingling

has replaced County Clerk Norman Goodman,
who ruled the courts for forty-five years,

including the eighteen it took me to raise my son.
You don't know me, Justice Tingling,

but I like the sound of your name,
I like the sound of Justice Anything,

you who refuse to honor exemptions
I have none of now.

The boy is no longer exempt, no,
and I want to serve, I want to make amends

for my absences,
my failures of civic duty.

I don't need to ask for time to raise him,
he's been raised, he no longer lives with me,

he's not waiting for me to come pick him up
to the sound of twenty questions

and the sound of the phone ringing and the dead dog barking.
He's a mystery to me,

old enough now for his own summons,
Justice Tingling, but he's not home

to receive it or fill it out,
he's not here to answer your questionnaire

about his own Good Conduct.
I listen to the traffic outside my window,

what would I do without it, it's a boon,
it croons,

it idled us through the days I tended
to the child who right at this moment

might be drinking his own lovely self
into a stupor

or watching the fraternity kids
drink themselves into stupors

in the basement and backrooms
of a self-replicating Upsilon Upsilon

across whose exterior in black poster paint
early one spring morning

someone spray-painted the words *rape haven*.
Anonymous, the papers said.

Anonymous, the brothers said
for the brother who is not my son, no,

my son has no brothers, Justice Tingling,
he's an only child, or he's only

a man now
who for all I know is or is not,

is or is not
with other young men

washing paint off a stone wall
with a high-powered hose and a stiff brush

like it never happened,
like it never happens.

Justice, forgive me.
Forgive me, Justice.

The Sky Flashes

Often when I'm in despair I turn to the back page
of the *New Yorker* and try to think up something
funny to say. The little drawings are so succinct
it can be hard to tell who's talking. Berryman's

Life, friends, is boring,
though recited by poets everywhere,
has probably been the winning caption
for no cartoon. Last summer I was so low

I ran out of magazines.
I got obsessed with entropy.
Is the world more closely allied with chaos
or with order? I asked everyone I love.

Chaos, my sister said, because she's a doctor.
Order, my mother said,
because she's an abstract expressionist.
I showed my father a cartoon

with a psychiatrist wearing a halo
and a man stretched out on the couch.
I'm afraid I can't help you with that one, he said,
and I was sure he'd win.

I told my sisters look, dad's ok, his mind still works,
he's still a funny man.
It took me all these months to realize
he was only answering me—

I'm afraid I can't help you with that one,
you, whoever you are.
I keep sending that caption in, every week,
hoping one day to win, one day soon,

before we lose him.
Truth is we ought to buy a book of jokes
and practice them over and over until we
perfect the hospice of it,

things are that bad.
My father's name is still funny,
one syllable, rhymes with *pain*.
Our friends used to call him *Pain*

and my mother *Wacky*, but I don't think
anyone could make me laugh right now.
If you'd laugh, I'd feel less alone.
Do you know my favorite joke,

about the man condemned to be hanged?
When the priest asks if he has anything
to say before they spring the trap, the man
says yes, this thing doesn't look safe.

Origin Story

When I was little I thought Karl Marx
was part of my extended family.
I assumed Groucho was, too,
because my mother had a passel of brothers
and before she was my mother she was a Marx.
The vice my uncles most effortlessly forgave was gullibility,
and who wouldn't want that in an ancestor?
The only real laughter comes from despair, Groucho said.
I intend to live forever or die trying, he said, which I've taken to heart.
I intend to cry forever or die laughing, said one version of this poem.
To laugh forever or die living, said another.
I intend to love forever—
Meanwhile, fires are burning again out west,
you can drive right through but who can stop them?
I grew up in California, and spent most of my childhood in a car
or a tent. Once my family camped out in Glacier National Park
and at a restaurant there I noticed people were leaving money
on tables, so I gathered it up. *Geworfenheit*
is a German term for being thrown into a game
without knowing the rules.
That pretty much explains it.
If only I could speak to whoever's in charge.
What would I ask for, if I could ask? Send up
a larger room! says one of my uncles in the stateroom scene.
Peace in the world, yes.
Clean air. Water. Less prejudice.
More intimacy, fewer lies.
Sometimes after sex my mind wanders
and the clock resets and I'm supposed to explain
into someone's armpit why I'm laughing.
Even I want to know.
Already it looks like we have to go soon,
you and I. But try.
Try to stay awhile longer.

Don't check your phone, the news, the various pages.
This is a page and you're still looking at it.
Your face is a page, as is mine.
Maybe numbered, maybe unnumbered.

Central Park

I'd like to buy one when I die,
one of the benches not yet spoken for,
not yet tagged with a small stainless plaque

and someone else's name.
If they're all gone, please,
help me carry a replica

to the boat pond so I can sit
and watch the model boats get nowhere
beautifully, rented by the fixed hours

I'm grateful not to be out of yet.
Another flicker of love,
an updated AAA membership,

and a handful of Pilot G-Tec-C4 blue-black pens,
what else do I need?
Universe,

watch over us.
Boat, my poor faraway father says,
as if my mother has never seen one.

Boat, he says, and we say, Yes,
aren't they beautiful.
Come winter,

the boathouse here is locked up,
the pond drained,
except one year it wasn't

and my son and I convinced ourselves
his new Golden Bright
could sail across.

Merry Christmas, no one said
as I pulled the black plastic liner bags
from the empty trash cans

and stepped into them,
one for each leg,
and waded into the addled water

to salvage the present.
I think that moment is something to remember,
or something to remember me by,

brief, vivid, foolhardy—
even the revenants watching from the line of benches
said so:

thus have been our travels.
Oblivion, they said,
there's no unenduring it.

Accursed Questions, iii

My friend asks if I ask questions to stay in control, but I'm just not into the cross-word puzzle or the Yankees or slow cooking or pornography, I don't know how to participate in the usual exchanges, so what is a loud noise you secretly like the sound of? I ask as we walk down the avenue and there I am controlling things again like I'm some kind of walking thermostat, or an intercom, yes, press mute and let me not hear doors slamming, not saying goodbye.

I love that sound especially, the sound of not saying goodbye turned all the way up loud, louder even than the trucks that shouted their way past us, louder than my friend who when it's time to go answers in his polite English murmur that he'd rather continue this discussion more discretely, upstairs, between the sheets.

I can't tell a joke but surely one of the best setups is how you men are always ready. What an appetite!

I rarely ask if you love me back or if you're there when the priest, the rabbi, and a juggler walk into the Vatican bar.

Will I ever admit my indiscretions?

Look for me in the heavenly bodies.

Or way up here on West 98th, stoned on negative capability, eating honeydew, taking these scholarly notes.

For example, the brain uses ten times more energy than any other body part.

Would we were octopuses, with brain cells in our arms!

In the most difficult logic problem on record, there are three gods, called True, False, and Random.

True always speaks truthfully, False always speaks falsely. But whether Random speaks truthfully or falsely is a completely random matter. The task is to determine their identities by asking three yes-no questions.

The gods understand English but answer in their own language.

Doctors agree I need to get laser holes made in my eyes. Laser pulses they call them. The pain will not be too great, they promise, though after it's over there's a chance I'll see more ghost images, nighttime halos around lights.

Go Back: You Are Going the Wrong Way say the highway signs in white lettering against a bright-red background.

I always wonder how they know which way we're headed.

The real question is not when but who, who will be there when you die?

Instead might I ask where you got your hat? I'd like to wear your hat—

And if it gets late again tonight, I might ask you the time, I might ask you a riddle or straighten my dress, I might commit a little crime or tell you the name of my press, My Body Up Against Yours, yes. My Body Up Against Yours Press.

To an event called "Poetry and the Creative Mind" I wore faux Spanx for the first time, discount Walgreens size L Spanx look-alike that kept me a little bit warm on a late April night. I was lonely when I took it off at home. I wonder if other women take theirs off in the bathroom before checking their faces and returning to the book, the bed, the optimistic erection.

————

Who put this old copy of *Jokes and Their Relation to the Unconscious* beneath my *Thesaurus*? Both titles obscured by dust.

Us, us—

the books so artlessly repercuss.

————

Tellisa wanted to know how to stop yelling. Ashley wanted to know what to do about her son's tantrums. Christina went awol. Barb got pregnant again and left with her son.

The mothers are young and on their own, disappointed or abused or simply left by their babyfathers. Can you skip me? one asks. We were making an inventory of apologies and questions:

Sorry, right?

It was two days after Valentine's Day.

Love is like the universe, could it be the tenth planet?

I'm sorry I missed it, what happened?

Pain Scale

Floating above the gynecologist's hands,
Dolor looks down at me
with her many expressions.

Someone sketched the eyes, the mouths,
someone pinned them up,
arranged the faces

so they softly say, like this? like this?
The doctor says to choose one,
but I'm no fool, I close my eyes

and the speculum is blind and cool,
widened and distracting.
Like the *Chikyū* vessel drilling

downhole from the ocean floor
into the untouched mantle,
it shows we're scarred inside

by what years and use and trespass do.
Every day the women open their eyes
and follow me into the streets,

the cities, like a wind murmur begins
a rumor of waves, the faces of earth
saying let this pain be error upon me writ.

In the Studio at End of Day

From my mother I've inherited dark eyes
and the desire to spend hours alone in a room
making things that might matter to no one.
She paints canvas after canvas, so many

she doesn't know what to do with them all.
Would you like one? Please,
come down to her studio,
she's giving them away now, as I write,

as I watch her and write and revise draft after draft
while not twenty feet from me she's spilling her paints
on the floor. She has more courage than I,
painting's not like writing, you can't get back

to earlier versions. Failure is hot right now,
said one of the children of her children,
and I think my mother was consoled.
I was, and then we were in it,

celebrating my mother and my father, both.
She made us laugh as she looked around the table
at the mutable world, her vast progeny—
so many of us she doesn't know what to do

with us all, and two already lost—
then raised a glass to my father
and their ninety years together.
Who's counting? Time passes

while my mother stands before the painting
as if it were a mirror
and paints the woman's face purple,
tilts the woman's head, blurs her outline.

She paints with whatever's at hand.
Chopsticks. Fingers. Elbow.
If she had a gun she'd use that.
My father built the storage racks

but there's no more room.
Try to hurry, try to get here fast,
before she leaves. Last night
she went home early,

and I was by myself in her studio,
which is like a womb. Everything
pulses. I turned the lights out
at the circuit breaker, as she taught me.

When they go off they make a kind of bang,
a shudder through the walls.
Tonight let's leave my mother
working here, she says she's not finished yet,

but take a painting on your way out
—tomorrow there will be another.
Read this draft, tomorrow there will be another.
Kiss her face.

Tomorrow there will be another.

433 Eros

An asteroid passed us by at 10 p.m. last night.
It was reported in the news.
What exactly is an asteroid?
A star of course I know, but an asteroid?
I've seen a few photos of 433 Eros,
where all the craters are named for famous lovers,
and the pictures are very sexy
even if it is just a minor planet
or the shattered remnant of a planetesimal.

Uncertainty Principle at the Atrium Bar

So much static in here,
and glasses clinking, laughter,
everyone talking a little louder

to make himself heard.
Is that why you're leaning so close
I can even from up here on the mezzanine

smell you smelling her?
Right now under this gauche chandelier
I'm not eavesdropping. Because if I were

would it change what's being said,
would it change what's floating from your lips
into the black hair flickering beside you?

I've never understood quantum mechanics
but I believe I should propel myself
far from here—

I'd earn a decent wage deciphering
sounds from another time and place,
from billions of miles and light-years ago,

sounds picked up in the exquisitely attuned
antennae of the Laser Interferometer
Gravitational-Wave Observatory.

Reports confirm the faraway arms
of the four-kilometer antennae
do nothing but translate waves into sound.

They drape themselves
over no one else's bare shoulders.
Have you listened to the LIGO recordings?

I play them again and again.
The universe!
Enormous duration

punctuated occasionally—
only a few times so far in my tenure here—
by what they call a chirp, a chirrup,

a transient signal that rises to middle C
and lasts only a fraction of a second easy to miss.
Yes, you are easy to miss.

Uncertainty Principle at Dawn

Come morning I'll make a list of obsessions
and maybe you won't still be on it,
only five-dollar bills, telescopes, anonymity,
waiting, beauty, silent comedy,
the silent comedy of beauty—
of waiting. Could I forswear

all these things and just crawl back
into the bed you and I once slept in?
What would happen then?
Play any film backward and it's elegy.
Play it fast-forward and it's a gas.

Beckett on the Jumbotron

Samuel Beckett, who to me is very fly,
may not fit everybody's definition of fly.

My own son, for example,
is not in love with Samuel Beckett,

he says he prefers Josh Beckett,
who used to play for the Sox.

He tries to explain the pleasures of baseball,
saying the game can go on forever,

there's no clock running down,
and I get that.

Some people want to live forever,
which would give us all time for more balks,

walks, no-hitters, daisy cutters, deep-in-the-counts.
To get through tonight's game

I brought *Waiting for Godot*
and already it sounds as if people are clapping

but the game's not over.
Look around—

The field is lit.
The crowd is lit.

It's all theater.
Up on the jumbotron they flash Beckett's pitching stats

and sometimes they flash live footage
of people in the far reaches of the stadium,

people who don't know they're being recorded.
I hope I show up there someday,

on the big screen!
With *Godot*,

with Lucky and Pozzo.
Look for us in the sky of pixels,

where the light gleams an instant,
then it's night once more—

Prayer for the Lost among Us

I wish we could let him
sleep all winter,
sleep all the way back to Elko,

Nevada, where forty years ago
we watched him take sleeping pills
and drink martinis

and pass out like a dead man
in the back of the station wagon
while we wandered the slot machines

and casino diners
wondering if he'd ever wake up.
We'd had a plan, then.

We'd agreed ahead of time
on a plan though we were too young
to give consent, wanting only

to please him, we were a little scared,
a little in awe,
you understand, he was our father.

When I look at him now
I see all of the fathers
he's been—

a funhouse mirror of fathers.
It's not a tragedy, my friend tells me,
and she's right.

The car was parked
far from the casino lights
and the plan was he'd wake up,

which he finally did, and we'd go to sleep
and he'd drive and drive
without having to listen to us

complain as the miles
passed beneath us on our
ongoing uncertain journey

into this gray morning.
Now we are the drivers,
he the sleeper who sleeps

standing up in the moonlight,
his legs cramping.
He the sleeper at the breakfast

table, folding and unfolding
his dirty paper napkin.
He the sleeper whose antacids

I wish we could replace
with sleeping pills and let him go to bed
without his oxygen mask

and fill his lungs with the mattress
where he sleeps beside my mother,
apart from this world.

His hair is the color of ashes
not yet set free upon the waters,
and his mouth is open,

the mouth of a gambler
who cannot speak
but shakes the dice in the glass,

the pills in his hand,
as if listening for something
and does not know why.

We had a plan for this
but he is not really here to enforce it,
and without him we lack the courage.

I was always afraid of his plans
and am relieved not to have to follow through,
relieved that only the pillows reproach us now

as I lay my head down
for another night as a child.

The Material World

As the writer signed his name he said the drug
was taking away his nouns, but his name is a proper noun
and there he was signing it. And his face is a proper noun's face,
and I was looking into it,
and his hand holding the pen above the book
was a series of shapely nouns existing in time and place,
which we were both occupying while *Dear Katherine*,
he wrote, which he corrected a moment later
by writing a large blue *C* over the capital *K*,
adding *Lovely to see you* under the salutation,
a play on words I understand only now.
Many hard years have passed since he wrote
in an earlier inscription
There must be an aesthetic besides death
with the same hand now closing the covers of his *New & Selected*,
a collection organized not by chronology
but by the alphabet, a more manageable affair.

Eternal Recurrence

I was no longer checked in under his name, Immortality,
but I'd do it all again, were we given such a thing.
Time is a monster, he'd whisper in my hair
before calling down for another hour.
Another hour after that and after that another hour.
As if the hours were ours to keep, to spend neverendingly.
He had to spell his name to the woman downstairs.
I am mortality, I can still hear him say
between kisses I remember to this day.

Accursed Questions, iv

I'm ready to try riddles, which apparently helped cure Henry VIII of dangerous melancholy, but the only one I remember is What did the zero say to the eight?

Nice belt could be the beginning of something and might for a few moments cure my melancholy.

Life, too, is dangerous.

Even days are dangerous. I'm serious. The ones around here can climb the apple tree and shake it to make the apples fall.

Sometimes my questions come out as if I were interrogating you, which is not my aim. My sister, who has the same upbringing, asks her questions gently.

My dog used to cock her head when I asked, You wanna go for a walk? Now she is ash on my ex's shelf.

In *King Lear, nothing* is often the answer. In Augustine's *Confessions, thou* is never far.

I don't think we're supposed to question God.

Into the Pacific crashed a plane years ago. They never found any piece of one of my sister's daughters and so there's the hope we try not to indulge that the girl is alive somewhere.

Is that you, I sometimes ask under my breath when I pass a beautiful child on the street, though of course she is no longer a child.

Is that you, I sometimes ask.

I am blue this morning. High winds again.

Get up, I tell myself, and then I say you need to sleep, look at you.

Should I lie on the floor here for ten minutes and sleep or storm ahead, some brief exhalations, these hands at the ends of these bent arms.

Tomorrow I'll go through the *when*'s and try to understand something more about time, which is at the heart of the sonnets, along with love.

‚‚‚

There are places in the world where people never ask riddles except when someone has died.

To be riddled with is to be made full of holes.

‚‚‚

Jean, in "Sanctuary," asks:

You   who I don't know   I don't know how to talk to you

—What is it like for you there?

‚‚‚

More than any other speech act, a question creates an other.

What are days for?

Days are where we live, writes Larkin. But who dreamed up this experiment? Are we in it or are we conducting it?

In clown class I was funny exactly once, when I walked through an imaginary square made out of four hats placed on the floor saying awful awful awful awful.

———

The only way to manage all this not-knowing is to hope in my next life everything will be clear, just wait. In the meantime, let me spend mornings here at Malecon, on 97th and Amsterdam, bent over these pages.

What are you writing, the Bible? the waiter asks. Why are you always working?

———

The novelist ordered a second glass of wine before he'd finished his first, a third before he'd finished his second. Red wine. Big steak. Two kinds of potatoes. Quite beautiful crooked hands. But what was he saying about sentences? Leave out the *and* if you're in a hurry. Solitude, and misery, may be necessary for a certain kind of work. You have to feel it first and if you've felt it you can just write the thing without explaining anything about it.

We said goodbye. We kissed on both cheeks. The subway wasn't working at that hour so I ran until I ran out of breath or the late-night bus stopped. Which was it? Which will it be? Solitude, misery, love?

———

Here in the city we have buses that kneel.

Amor Fati

What do you need? the Quiet Man asked
when I knocked again at his door.

What do you want?
He was closing up.

I don't know, I said.
Woolf, Anbesol, Baldwin, Keats,

I'll take anything.
I knew sometimes he slept right there in his shop,

with blankets on the bottom shelf,
history above, *Bulletin*

of the Atomic Scientists to the left.
Papers littered his desk

and the floor where we lay our heads,
letting the pure products of the shapely mind

inform the equally combustible body.
Who is it who says the closer you are

to an irreversible apocalypse the more fragile
language is?

We slid the dictionaries from the shelves
and opened them to *apocalypse*,

the word on everyone's lips.
O lips!—

As if we could ever bid these joys farewell.

_____

95

Notes

The Amenities
Lines in this poem borrow from Sylvia Plath's "The Applicant" and "Death & Co." and from Gwendolyn Brooks's "An Aspect of Love, Alive in the Ice and Fire."

En Route
Saint Catherine's head, separated from her body, is in the Basilica Cateriniana San Domenico, Siena.

An Apprehension
This poem quotes Kafka's "Investigations of a Dog," Elizabeth Bishop, and Jean Valentine. With thanks to Royal Security.

The Skin of the Face Is That Which Stays Most Naked, Most Destitute
The title of this poem is from Emmanuel Levinas.

Epistemology
Wonderful facts about trees drawn from Peter Wohlleben's *The Hidden Life of Trees*. Lines 14 to 16 borrow definitions from dictionaries etymological and otherwise.

Still Life
L'Origine du monde was painted by Gustave Courbet in 1866 and hangs in the Musée d'Orsay.

Lyric and Narrative Time at Café Loup
This poem borrows from Wisława Szymborska's poem "The Century's Decline" (tr. Stanisław Barańczak and Clare Cavanagh). Thanks and credit to Mark Doty for his insights on time.

Accursed Questions, i
"He will never ride the red horse she describes" is from "Questions Are Remarks" by Wallace Stevens. This section of "Accursed Questions" (and others) borrows from Philip Larkin's "Days"; Jean Valentine's *Lucy*; and Augustine's *Confessions* (tr. Edward B. Pusey).

Idée Fixe
With thanks to Pence Orchards.

Essay on *An Essay Concerning Human Understanding*
This poem owes a debt to John Locke's *An Essay Concerning Human Understanding* and to Claire Monin, whose intensive French courses I highly recommend (www .francepass.fr). If you want to spend a night in adoration at the Sacré-Coeur, you have to let them know in advance. Please wear a helmet if you hire a bicycle in Paris, even if no one else does.

Son in August
This poem owes a debt to Rilke's "Archaic Torso of Apollo."

The Necessary Preoccupations
Lines in this poem echo Shakespeare's *The Tempest* via Eliot's *The Waste Land*.

The Art of the Security Question
This poem was informed by "Your Mother's Maiden Name Is Not a Secret" by Anne Diebel, published in the *New York Times*, 28 December 2017. The full title of Nina Simone's song is "Ain't Got No, I Got Life." *Call Me by Your Name* is a film directed by Luca Guadagnino based on André Aciman's novel.

O Esperanza!
This poem quotes from Richard Rorty's "Anticlericalism and Atheism," published in *The Future of Religion* by Richard Rorty and Gianni Vattimo, ed. Santiago Zabala (2005).

Accursed Questions, ii
This text borrows (as many poems in this collection do) from Samuel Beckett's play *Happy Days*. "Agitated by the phenomena of hours" is slightly misquoted from but fully in debt to Beckett's *Proust*. I have lost the source for the idea about eros existing in the space between interlocutor and addressee; apologies.

The Humanities
This poem is written against the endless and unacceptable acts of racial violence in the United States. The last stanzas owe a deep debt to Dianne Wiest for her performance in Beckett's *Happy Days* and incorporate lines from that play.

Calamity Jane on Etsy after the 2016 Election
With a debt to Frank O'Hara's "Poem [Lana Turner has collapsed!]."

Another Divine Comedy
The kickscooter is manufactured by Xootr; ask for Steve if you call the manufacturer directly, and mention my name.

Let Facts Be Submitted to a Candid World
The title of this poem is a direct quote from the Declaration of Independence. There are also echoes of Elizabeth Bishop, Wallace Stevens, and Larry Levis.

Metaphor on the Crosstown
This poem quotes Robert Lowell's "Epilogue."

Summons
Justice Milton Tingling was sworn in as County Clerk of New York County in 2015, replacing Norman Goodman.

The Sky Flashes
The title of this poem comes from John Berryman's "Dream Song 14," as does the quoted line.

Origin Story
The stateroom scene referred to in this poem is from the Marx Brothers' film *A Night at the Opera.*

Central Park
You can adopt a bench through the New York City Central Park Conservancy ("Official Caretakers of Central Park"). The pleasures of Pilot G-Tec-C4 pens were introduced to me by Joshua Beckman and I have used them ever since. The idea of speaking directly to the universe comes from Dana Levin. Golden Bright is the name of a company that makes radio-controlled boats. This poem echoes Elizabeth Bishop's "Over 2,000 Illustrations and a Complete Concordance."

Accursed Questions, iii
The "most difficult logic problem" was presented by logician George Boolos and published in 1996; Boolos credits the logician Raymond Smullyan with devising the problem, quoted here in truncated form. For more than twenty years, the Children's Museum of Manhattan has run an early literacy program for mothers and their young children residing in the New York City shelter system; the last section of "Accursed Questions, iii" quotes the women as they were writing a collaborative poem.

Pain Scale

The pain scale in at least one gynecologist's office has realistic women's faces rather than the more common cartoon faces. The *Chikyū* is a Japanese research ship that can drill miles into the earth's mantle, farther than any other science drilling vessel. One of the stated aims of the expeditions is to look for "clues about the origin and evolution of early life on earth." This poem is indebted to Elizabeth Bishop's "Filling Station" and Alice Oswald's *Memorial*, which it cites. The last line of the poem borrows indirectly from Shakespeare's Sonnet 116.

Uncertainty Principle at the Atrium Bar

The Heisenberg Uncertainty Principle states that phenomena are changed by the act of being observed. There are two Laser Interferometer Gravitational-Wave Observatories. In February 2016 LIGO recorded the sound of two black holes colliding in a distant galaxy more than a billion light-years ago.

Beckett on the Jumbotron

The last two lines of the poem are spoken by Pozzo in Act II of Samuel Beckett's *Waiting for Godot*.

Prayer for the Lost among Us

This poem owes a debt to Larry Levis's "The Cry."

Accursed Questions, iv

Jean Valentine's poem "Sanctuary" was published in her fourth collection, *The Messenger*.

Amor Fati

The *Bulletin of the Atomic Scientists* is both a publication and a nonprofit organization that tracks scientific advancements in order to educate the public, guide policy, and protect the planet and its inhabitants. The *Bulletin* created the Doomsday Clock ("a universally recognized indicator of the world's vulnerability to catastrophe from nuclear weapons, climate change, and new technologies emerging in other domains"). The "pure products" are stolen from William Carlos Williams. "As if we could ever bid these joys farewell" is a variation on a line from John Keats's "Sleep and Poetry."

Acknowledgments

Thanks to the editors of the following journals, series, and anthologies for publishing these poems (sometimes in different versions or with different titles):

The Academy of American Poets Poem-A-Day Series, "Comic Morning" and "Epistemology"

The American Poetry Review, "Central Park," "The Humanities," and "In the Studio at End of Day"

The Bennington Review, "Summons" and "The Necessary Preoccupations"

Green Mountains Review, "Landscape with Borrowed Contours"

Harper's Magazine, "Pain Scale"

The Literary Review, "Beckett on the Jumbotron," "The Light from across the Fields," "Lore," "Still Life," and "The Skin of the Face Is That Which Stays Most Naked, Most Destitute"

The New Yorker, "Essay on *An Essay Concerning Human Understanding*" and "Son in August"

The New York Review of Books, "The Sky Flashes"

Ploughshares, "Lyric and Narrative Time at Café Loup"

Poetry, "An Apprehension," and "Idée Fixe"

Poetry International, "The Amenities," "Forensics," "Let Facts Be Submitted to a Candid World," "Calamity Jane on Etsy after the 2016 Election," "Appeal to Numbers," "The Material World," and "Amor Fati"

The Spectator, "Eternal Recurrence"

Tin House, "Prospectus" and "O Esperanza!"

"O Esperanza!" also appears in *The Best American Poetry 2016*, edited by Edward Hirsch, with series editor David Lehman (Scribner, 2016).

For their generosity, acumen, and friendship, deep thanks to Andrew Boynton, Jericho Brown, Miranda Field, Ed Hirsch, Ilya Kaminsky, Nick Laird, Deborah Landau, Alessandra Lynch, El Malecon, Donna Masini, Michael Morse, Dennis Nurkse, Helen Schulman, Tom Sleigh, Jean Valentine, Ellen Bryant Voigt, David Wells, Abby Wender, Dianne Wiest, Fiona Wilson, and Matthew Zapruder. Immeasurable appreciations to Saskia Hamilton, for her unerring compass. (What wisdom can you find that is greater than kindness? asked the painter Henri Rousseau.)

For his patience, wit, and discerning green pen, gratitude to my editor Jeff Shotts. ("Ignore Jeff," he once wrote in the margin, which I did just that once.)

Inexpressible thanks to my mother and father, for their love. And to my son, for his steady heart and good humor.

CATHERINE BARNETT is the author of *Into Perfect Spheres Such Holes Are Pierced* and *The Game of Boxes*, winner of the James Laughlin Award of the Academy of American Poets. Her honors include a Whiting Award and a Guggenheim Fellowship. She is a member of the core faculty of New York University's Creative Writing Program, a Distinguished Lecturer at Hunter College, and an independent editor in New York City.

The text of *Human Hours* is set in Bembo. Composition by
Bookmobile Design and Digital Publisher Services, Minneapolis,
Minnesota. Manufactured by Versa Press on acid-free,
30 percent postconsumer wastepaper.